DEAR BRUNO

Alice Trillin

Illustrated by Edward Koren

THE NEW PRESS / NEW YORK

LIBRARY OF CONGRESS CATALOGUING-IN-PUBLICATION DATA

Trillin, Alice Stewart.
 Dear Bruno/Alice Trillin: illustrated by Edward Koren.
  p.   cm.
 SUMMARY: In this letter to a friend's son who has just been
 diagnosed with cancer the author shares her own experience
 with a tumor and offers a listening heart.
   ISBN 1-56584-057-7 (hardcover)
   1. Cancer—Juvenile literature. 2. Tumors in children—
 Juvenile literature. 3. Navasky, Bruno—Health.
 [1. Cancer. 2. Tumors. 3. Diseases. 4. Letters. 5. Navasky, Bruno.]
 I. Koren, Edward, ill. II. Title.
 RC264. T75 1988
 618.92'994—dc20   95-42320
                                                   CIP
                                                   AC

Published in the United States by The New Press, New York
Distributed by W. W. Norton & Company, Inc., New York

ESTABLISHED IN 1990 AS A MAJOR ALTERNATIVE TO THE LARGE,
COMMERCIAL PUBLISHING HOUSES, THE NEW PRESS IS A FULL-SCALE
NONPROFIT AMERICAN BOOK PUBLISHER OUTSIDE OF THE UNIVERSITY PRESSES.
THE PRESS IS OPERATED EDITORIALLY IN THE PUBLIC INTEREST,
RATHER THAN FOR PRIVATE GAIN; IT IS COMMITTED TO PUBLISHING,
IN INNOVATIVE WAYS, WORKS OF EDUCATIONAL, CULTURAL, AND COMMUNITY VALUE
THAT, DESPITE THEIR INTELLECTUAL MERITS, MIGHT NOT NORMALLY
BE COMMERCIALLY VIABLE. THE NEW PRESS'S EDITORIAL OFFICES
ARE LOCATED AT THE CITY UNIVERSITY OF NEW YORK.

Book design by HALL SMYTH/GORDON WHITESIDE
Production management by KIM WAYMER
Printed in the UNITED STATES OF AMERICA

9 8 7 6 5 4 3 2 1

to the kids at
THE HOLE IN THE WALL GANG CAMP

and to their special friends

PAUL NEWMAN
and JOANNE WOODWARD

Young people who have or have had cancer are a very special bunch. I watch them and swear they carry themselves differently. Even the youngest of them seems to know something that I don't. They have a grace that I envy.

It is all apparent in this book: a letter written to a young boy with cancer by a young woman who had survived it. I especially note that it was written in the service of the child and not to glorify its author.

There is patience and generosity, wonderfully relaxed humor, sensible instruction, and, I am happy to note, no sufferance at all for idiots. Edward Koren's ink sketches capture my sentiments exactly.

Paul Newman

Nova Scotia, Canada
August 2, 1979

Dear Bruno,

Bud has already written and told you all our jokes
(not quite—did you hear the one about the fog?—
oh well, it's probably too dense for you) and he has
told you about what happens in Nova Scotia in the summer,
and he has sent you an arrow-through-the-head to wear
when you tell the doctors you have a little headache,
and so I thought that there wasn't much left for me to write
you, but there is one thing I know about that Bud doesn't
know about, and that is what it is like to have a tumor
in your lung.

Did you hear the one about the fog?

As you probably know, I had one too, just three years ago, at about this time of year. Mine was an adenocarcinoma, not a Brunoma (is that how you spell it?), and somewhat different from yours, but I did have radiation, and some chemotherapy, and surgery, and even something called immunotherapy, so I know a little bit about some of the things that are happening to you and some of the things that might happen. I know that when I was sick, I wanted very badly to talk to someone who had the same thing I had, and there was no one (though since then I have met a lot of people who have had lung tumors) so I thought you might want to talk to me or to ask me some things. Doctors don't always know exactly what it feels like to have the things they do done to you.

Doctors don't always know exactly what it feels like
to have the things they do done to you.

A re you having radiation now? The main thing I remember about radiation was the awful Muzak they played while they were zapping me. It always started just at the moment when the enormous steel door slammed shut, as if slamming the door turned on the music at the same time it turned on the rays.

The radiologists were very nice, but they always seemed to want to talk to me about real estate. They were having trouble evicting the tenants next door so they would have room for the new CAT scanner. I don't suppose your radiologist talks to you about real estate. That's one of the advantages of being twelve.

The radiologists were very nice.

Is the radiation making you feel sick? I never could tell if it made me feel sick, because it was summer in New York and about one hundred degrees, and that never makes me feel too great. At one point I got a bit over-radiated in my esophagus and couldn't swallow very well and could only eat banana milkshakes. I had trouble explaining to Abigail and Sarah why I didn't have to eat any vegetables or fruit in order to get dessert.

Is the radiation making you feel sick?

I hear that you had to have almost every test and scan they have to offer in that place. Having tests seemed to me about the worst thing about being in the hospital, even worse than surgery. (Which, by the way, wasn't all that bad, surprisingly. If you have to have it, be sure to talk to me first.) The thing I hated about tests was all the time you have to spend in the hall waiting to have them. The tests never seemed quite as bad as the waiting. (I did have a bone marrow biopsy given by a doctor with one arm in a sling—his barbecue had flared up and burned him—and that was a bit scary.)

It's nothing! My barbecue flared up and burned me!

The thing that always astonished me was how incredibly well-behaved I was, even when I had to wait in hallways until I thought I'd been abandoned, and was sure that all the doctors had left for the weekend. You get conditioned into being very well-behaved and polite, saying things like, "Excuse me, but I think I have been forgotten because I have been sitting here for three hours and my intravenous bottle dripped dry two hours ago." And then they say, "Oh dear, sorry, but all the doctors have left for the weekend." (Actually, that never really quite happened, but it seemed about to many times.)

*I thought I'd been abandoned, and was sure that all the doctors
had left for the weekend.*

The other thing I remember very well is occasionally being very angry that I had to be sick while everyone else I knew was well. After all, I am a reasonably nice person, had always done my best to behave myself, and there were all sorts of awful people wandering around perfectly healthy on those lovely summer days while I had to lie in bed having tubes and needles stuck into me.

Why me?

My doctor said that getting sick like that— getting a lung tumor when you haven't smoked and when you are way too young to get one—is like having a flower pot drop on your head while you are walking down the street. It really isn't your fault, and there isn't much you can do about it except try to get the flower pot off your head and go on walking.

What you really want most of all is to get back to doing the very trivial, dumb things that you always do. Most of all I wanted to come to Nova Scotia and plant my garden peas. Well, after a long while I did, and this year I have the best crop of peas I've ever had.

The other day while I was picking peas I started thinking about something that happened a couple of months ago when I gave a speech to some medical students about what it was like to be a patient. At the end of the speech, one of the students asked me an incredible question. He said, if I knew that I would be OK, that I wouldn't be sick again, and if I could choose, would I choose to have been sick, to have gone through the experience I had gone through, as awful as it had been. I looked at him, stunned. That was a secret. I had never said it out loud. Of course, I would never choose to have cancer—that's just silly—but you don't get to choose, and the secret he had guessed was that there were things about having had cancer that I liked.

This year I have the best crop of peas I've ever had!

I won't try to convince you that there will ever be anything about having cancer that you like—except maybe banana milkshakes. I will just tell you that I know things now that I could never have known, and I am a different person now, different in ways that I like. There is a great line in a play by Shakespeare called *King Lear:* "Ripeness is all." Now this is said when the king has been out on the heath in a big storm and is going crazy and two out of three of his daughters have deserted him. It seems to me that there ought to be an easier way to get ripe—you ought to be able to read a book or something. It must be very hard for you to see anything at all good about what is happening to you. And it sounds stupid for me to say that there is. But some day, when you are better — and riper — we should talk about it. The one thing I know is that you and I will know some things that other people don't know, and we will have a lot to talk about.

Ripeness is all.

Don't forget, if there is anything you want to ask, or just talk about, please call. I'll see you when we get back to New York. Give my love to your Mom and Dad.

Love, Alice

KOREN

October 2, 1995

Dear Alice,

Thanks for your letter.

I really should have answered sooner, but I've been so busy. After you wrote to me, I made a list of everything I wanted to do when I left the hospital, and then suddenly I was doing it.

There was high school to finish, then college. For a few years, I was living in Japan. I even did some hitchhiking (but don't tell my parents!). Now I'm busy writing poetry, and climbing mountains all across America.

Thanks again for cheering me up. Don't forget to tell Bud about me climbing the mountains. Oh, nevermind, it's probably over his head.

Love, Bruno

Author's Note

MY LETTER TO BRUNO BECAME A BOOK AFTER
I came across it by chance a few weeks before my
husband and I were going to be volunteer
counselors at The Hole In The Wall Gang Camp,
a camp for children who have cancer or serious
blood diseases. It occurred to me that I might be
able to use the letter with the kids at camp if I
could convince my friend Ed Koren to make some
drawings to go along with it. Ed enthusiastically
agreed, Caroline Maillot of the *New Yorker* art
department generously contributed layout and
color Xerox assistance, and my daughter Abigail
helped me glue the original version of this book
together the night before we left for camp.

SNUGGLED ON A BUNK AT REST HOUR, I READ
"Dear Bruno" to some of the ten-year old girls in
my cabin. Amazingly, one of my campers had had
a neuroblastoma, a tumor closely related to the
neuroepithelioma Bruno named a "Brunoma."
She told me, rather matter-of-factly, that she was
one of the rare children to survive this particularly virulent form of cancer, and I was pleased
to be able to introduce her to Bruno, whose
experience had been so much like hers. Reading
"Dear Bruno" with my campers led to conversations that I will remember forever. The children
who read the book urged me to publish it, so,
of course, it is dedicated to them and all of the
children at the extraordinary Hole In The Wall
Gang Camp.

I HAD NEVER BEEN IN A CANCER HOSPITAL BEFORE
the day in July of 1976 when I went to Memorial
Sloan-Kettering Cancer Center to begin post-
surgery treatment. I was terrified. As I rode in
the elevator to my appointment, a kid of about
fifteen, who I assumed had leukemia because he
had no hair, asked me what kind of cancer I had.
When I told him I had lung cancer, he smiled
and said, "They treat that like the common cold
around here." That was the cheeriest thing
anyone had said to me since the ominous shadow
had been spotted in my lung a few weeks earlier,
and that young man's words set the tone for the
countless visits I have made to that amazing
hospital over the past nineteen years. As I stood
in the blood count line every week in the months

that followed, as I listened to the jokes exchanged and the stories told—what I described as cancer patients' "brave talk"—I began to feel that I was listening to conversations at gatherings of knights who had just slain some particularly fierce dragons.

IN RE-READING THE LETTER I WROTE TO BRUNO, at a distance of sixteen years, I recognized its tone as that of the young man I met in the elevator that morning and of my companions in all of those blood count lines. It is also the tone I heard in the voices of many of the children at The Hole In The Wall Gang Camp. (The message on one of their baseball caps read "Cancer Sucks.") Someone who hasn't heard those voices might make the mistake of thinking that knights who talk "brave talk" and make jokes about dragons don't understand how truly dangerous dragons are. But the bravest knights, having fought the fiercest battles, understand the nature of dragons better than anyone.

THOSE OF US WHO HAVE HAD CANCER, UNLIKE real knights, also know that even after our own fierce battles the dragon might not be dead, but only sleeping. Perhaps it is finding out that we can live with this knowledge and still relish such delights as garden peas, skateboards, and summer camp that makes us ripe. There are worse things to be than a fighter-of-dragons.

ALICE TRILLIN
Nova Scotia, Canada
August 1995